The Creed

of the

Conquering Chief

As expounded by the
Inspired Orator

———

An Experiment in Psychology

———

Written down by
ALBERT LEWIS PELTON

———

1926
THE RALSTON UNIVERSITY PRESS
MERIDEN, CONN.

J. F. TAPLEY CO.
NEW YORK

THE PROFESSOR'S PROLOGUE.

(Last evening, at the Psychic Arts Auditorium, a lecture of striking power and scientific importance, was delivered under rather unusual circumstances.

Today I called upon the Professor and asked if he would tell me how he came to discover and apply his principle of "induced inspration." His story, as well as the lecture itself, follows).

— AUTHOR'S NOTE.

THE PROFESSOR'S PROLOGUE.

Man is the crowning work of the Maker of all created things.

He gains his greatness and maintains his position of supremacy, solely because he possesses that wonderful endowment: MIND—the ability to think and reason; and having thought—to forge ahead along such lines as he chooses.

He is forever separated from—and superior to—all other orders of creation, because no other has this "Mind" attribute.

* * * * * * *

For many years I have been an investigator in that great field of phenomena known as Psychology—the study of the Human mind.

In my studies and researches into the Science of mental power, my experiments had been largely in the realm commonly termed Genius.

Genius is the classification given certain men who exhibit rare qualities of mind-power. It is used to describe the sort of men who concentrate and intensify to the nth degree, phases of brain energy which the mass of men use only in a weak, scattering way.

"The highest form of creation, whether in art or life, is genius" says Wingfield-Stratford. "Genius is natural to man, and in no way more mysterious than any other faculty of the mind. It may be defined as subconscious activity functioning rightly."

Men of Genius are unmistakable guide-posts where History records man's passage from the beginning to the end of world-life. Men of genius are stately peaks rising above the foothills covered by the submerged multitudes.

I had sought to discover the causes or secret—the foundation principle, as it were—of the great man. Time after time I had mentally asked myself:

1. *Are there any definite laws which the superior man applies?*

2. *Is "Genius" a divine endowment—the despair of all to whom it does not come early and clearly in life?*

3. *Are men of genius a "race apart"—each one struck off from the Great Center only at odd intervals?*

Those were some of the questions for which I tried to find answers in my mind. They caused much thought and meditation. In whatever direction I pursued my quest for some tangible result—always was it made manifest that the genius-mind exemplified these deep truths:

1. Thought *intensified.*

2. Vision *made concrete.*

3. Clear observation *frozen into fact.*

In short—it is Mind-power turned into ACTION. Genius is energy-charged, Will-directed Thought-force *vitalized into life.* This is the turning point at which the man of genius separates himself from the humdrum crowd.

Thought is Power!

Again and again declare that great truth. Believe it. Dream it. Go forth and PUT IT INTO ACTION.

Ah yes!—ability to *think*—that is the great man's chief characteristic. It is Brain-energy harnessed and made productive; it is the trait which infallibly makes men masters.

I have watched men at work and men at play. I have studied the mass—the so-called "submerged millions"—and their minds grow little more than weeds. Their brains are giving them scant harvests. Something has blighted and stunted their productiveness. Their brain plants seem to have scarcely enough depth or root to save them from blowing across the sands— withering and disappearing.

And they constitute the bulk of mankind!

Yet again—here and there I have seen men whose minds were productive to a remarkable degree. Deep, fertile, steadily reaching upwards—self-centered, sturdy and strong. They owned brains which were yielding rich fruits of thought—a Mind in all its greatness.

The Mind has two levels or phases of action. The upper or surface level which often reveals beautiful creations and hangs heavy with rich and luscious fruits —those wonderful products of mental growth and harvest. The lower level—that deep, unfathomable sea— is where the surface life roots down and from which it draws its nourishment and power.

These two levels of the Mind are given the names *conscious* and *sub-conscious*. The mind-life of which we are aware in the round of the day's duties, is the Conscious phase of mind. Deep down below the surface, there exists a vast mental life of which we are not aware. It is the sub-conscious realm—the powerhouse of Thought-energy.

It is from these depths that men of genius draw a brimming measure of creative power. It is from this unfailing spring the great man brings up into conscious use, the huge stores of thought or idea-force

which he turns into visible ACTION or RESULTS.
Then men call him "genius".

The relation of the conscious mind to the sub-conscious (under) mind, might be illustrated in this way:
after a heavy rain storm you will find the ground still
damp or wet on the surface. But deeper and deeper
down—trickling through the grains of sand—the *bulk*
of the rain has passed, finally to accumulate far below
the surface, awaiting the call of the artesian drill.

Such a reservoir is your sub-conscious mind. During
your waking hours it is incessantly receiving a supply
of thought material from the upper or conscious mind.
It is storing, combining, mixing, increasing and amassing BRAIN-POWER. All that you have ever seen,
heard or felt has sunk down into your subconscious
storehouse. It is almost as Prof. Babbage has said:
"The air is one vast library, on whose pages are forever
written all that man has ever said, or woman whispered."

Great is he who has learned the secret of making
the sub-conscious yield up its unlimited wealth. HE
IS A GENIUS.

* * * * * * *

I asked of many I met: *"What is the secret of
reaching this great reservoir of Power? How can this
sub-conscious mind be tapped in the way the genius
draws upon it? How can the average man command
this creative force in a masterly fashion?"*

And always did those who had given the subject any
thought reply *"O, genius is just 'inspiration', that's
all,"* or words to that effect. Others said: *"Genius is
the result of hard work".*

To be a genius one need only study hard enough to
be able to tell the people what they already think.

The superiority of genius is therefore no different from that of any educated person; *except in the degree of application.* Anyone might possess this superiority.

People seem to hold the common belief that the great man is a peculiar personality, unsolvable excepting on the ground of a divine "inspiration" having aroused his every cell and fibre and nerve—and made him what he is.

Therefore my problem resolved into this question: "What is 'inspiration,' so called?"

I say: **Inspiration is a Mind a-flame.**

Inspiration is a Heart a-glow.

Inspiration is a Body a-tingle.

Inspiration, as explaining the great man's secret, is nothing else than energy from the sub-conscious mind flaring up into the field of the conscious mind—and rapidly ripening fruits or products which astonish the average person.

I have seen men at their work—dull, listless, mentally asleep. "Nobody at home" as the expression is. And again, here and there I have seen another kind of man, in whom was pulsating a vibrant Life-energy—a Mind-energy—a Creative energy. He is eager, ambitious, alert, and alive in every cell. His very soul seems to be peering out of his eye-windows—beaming in every action and effort to express his true Self. It is to men of this type that "inspiration" comes as a spark which flashes into action the gift of greatness.

"God creates by intuition; man creates by inspiration, strengthened by observation. This second creation, which is nothing else but divine action carried out by man, is what is called genius".

What, then, is the secret of this inspirational spark? To solve this question called for deep thought, careful test and close observation. I confess that even now I have found no universal, good-for-all formula. I fear that none ever will be found. The training, the goals, the heritage and the lives of men are so widely different, that each must find his own special route.

But I have been told that what I did find, and teach, has been of priceless help in many lives—and such as it is I give it freely in the pages that follow.

* * * * * * *

I will here set forth how I came to conduct the psychological experiment which forms the chief part of this treatise. There was a young man of my acquaintance who represented the high type of man pictured a few paragraphs back. He was ambitious, bright; he was a zealous student of life—and frequently possessed of a burning desire to do BIG THINGS.

One evening I invited him to my study. I explained some of the fundamental principles upon which the human mind acted. I propounded my theories. I pointed out that any man, barring actual mental weaklings, was capable of rich thought, creative intellect and endowed with powers to do what is usually termed "phenomenal thinking." But I also made it clear that most of us, alas, allow this quality of genius to slumber, to weaken, and to fade away. We go through life unaware of what we might do, of the high goals we might reach, of the brilliant accomplishments really open to us, of the masses of men we might lead—and the success-heights to which we might rise.

All, in the last analysis, because we are too "indolent" to make the glorious attempt.

I told him that with his permission and co-operation, I wished to bring into action, if possible, the so-called mental state "Inspiration." It would be a quickening of his brain powers into a creative, forceful, brilliant mind-machine.

I asked him if he knew of any sense-stimulus that seemed to make his mind increase its flow of ideas— any external influence that caused a sort of mental thrill and a concentration of his powers.

The young man said that on several occasions he had listened to the rippling notes of a sweet-toned music box, and that at such times a new world of possibility seemed to open to him; that at such times ambition seemed to well up from the depths of his being and urge him to make magnificent advances.

That was enough!

The secret of the sense-stimulus which opened the road to *his* "genius centre" was clear. With his co-operation I felt assured I could carry through an experiment in psychology that would be of genuine interest. As a scientific explanation of how it was to be produced has considerable bearing upon the actual results achieved, I will give a brief analysis.

*   *   *   *   *   *   *

While listening to the tones which stirred his greater ambitions the young man, mentally, was in an exalted state between consciousness and un-consciousness—he was verging on a borderland state allied to sleep—but not precisely the same. In our dreams we often do great things; sometimes we are kings and leaders. Sometimes we are builders of wonderful estates. This is because in sleep the conscious mind—the mind which scarcely dares think of greatness as a POSSESSED FACT—is stilled. The dominant do-all and be-all subconscious mind then has full sway. Oh that we might learn to express more of this sub-conscious mind in our waking hours!

Now, then, what I sought to do was to get his mind into such a condition that it was on the delicate balancing point between the conscious and the unconscious states::—all the while keeping his "upper" mind in condition to interpret the "under" mind's messages. I wanted to get a *concrete record* of what was being brought up from the mental reservoirs or mind-storage center.

My plan was to give a public demonstration of my theory, and accordingly the following announcement appeared in the local press:

EXPERIMENT IN PSYCHOLOGY
Friday Evening, October 30
PSYCHIC ARTS AUDITORIUM

An experiment in practical psychology will be made, in an attempt to have a young man demonstrate the deeper powers of the Human Mind—its Creative Ability and Genius Qualities.

In the role of an Inspired Orator he will deliver the lecture

THE CREED OF THE CONQUERING CHIEF

Nothing like it has ever before been tried. Everybody interested in the advancement of Psychic Research is invited.

Immediately I began to prepare the young man's mind for the test. It was not to be an illustration of hypnotism, for in that state the subject does only what the operator directs: voluntary action is for the time being suspended. My experiment would leave the young man full mental control of himself. What I sought to accomplish was to bring the subconscious or "under mind" into unusually close touch with the conscious state of mind.

He came to my study every evening and I instructed him to let his mind and thought be receptive to my directions. They were purely "suggestion" as generally understood and were along the following lines:

"You are to appear before an audience on Friday Evening. You will be calm, cool and collected. You will be poised in manner. You will have no hesitation nor fear. You will be master of the situation. You are to advance forward on the stage, easily, thoughtfully and quietly, as the tones of your favorite—the beautiful Evening Symphony—reach you. You are to feel the old thrill of ambition—the sense of greatness, the desire for leadership. You are to let your thoughts soar—you have often done this in the quiet of your home. Now you are to give actual utterance to what you see and hear and feel. You are to be aware, in a general way, of your surroundings. But more than this: *you are to let your subconscious mind pour forth unrestrained.*"

"You are to deliver the inspired lecture 'THE CREED OF THE CONQUERING CHIEF.' You are to say everything at your command that has a bearing on this subject—if you wish, quote from other thinkers along this line. Understand—you are to address this audience on the subject 'The Creed of the Conquering Chief."

"You will become fired with Ambition—your brain will create principles and rules which underlie the philosophy of the Creed of Conquest—the Art of WIN-

NING in every legitimate phase of life. You are to
remember that the human mind, divine spark glowing
in it, creates from time to time, superhuman works.
You are to sink below the level of ordinary consciousness and draw out rich thoughts from your intellectual
storehouse. You are to believe and *will* that this treasure is to come within your reach."

"You are to deliver the inspired lecture "𝕿𝖍𝖊 𝕮𝖗𝖊𝖊𝖉
𝖔𝖋 𝖙𝖍𝖊 𝕮𝖔𝖓𝖖𝖚𝖊𝖗𝖎𝖓𝖌 𝕮𝖍𝖎𝖊𝖋.""

*   *   *   *   *   *   *

And so, each evening I instructed him—clearly,
forcefully, directly. I could see that it was sinking
in. There's a glow in men's eyes that tells rare tales—
if only one will observe closely. His were telling me
of what the subconscious mind was accumulating. By
Wednesday evening I knew—or could estimate fairly
well—that his brain was quickening for the birth of
the oration. For down in this "under mind" wonderful things take place, of which we are not often aware.
It knows, sees, hears, thinks and unfolds a vast life
story which seldom rises to where we can record it.
I was to make the form of inspiration which loosened
his sub-conscious gates to let out new values.

On Friday evening a somewhat curious though intelligent and friendly audience filled the Auditorium.
The young man came to me in a retiring room at the
rear of the stage shortly before the time set for the
lecture. He was controlled and at ease—and seemed
eager to go ahead with the experiment. He assured
me that he had done much active thinking and had
picked up a number of gems from different sources.
But he also believed his sub-conscious mind was to
utter a rich amount of "food for thought."

At the time announced, I stepped before the audience and briefly outlined my plan, and what I hoped to demonstrate. I stated that there were ways of stimulating the human brain or Mind to a much greater degree of Creativeness than was generally practiced. What was universally needed was that each individual find the key for his peculiar sub-conscious lock. This young man when stimulated by a certain form of music, was aroused, mentally, to a high degree of mental power. It was practically the so-called *"inspiration"* which was said to explain the secret of genius. I asked for the utmost consideration on the part of the audience and retired.

The exquisite harmonies of the Evening Symphony began and the young man advanced to the center of the stage. Gradually the tones died away and he began this address:

THE CREED
OF THE
CONQUERING CHIEF

As delivered by the Inspired Orator

---

*"The World Remembers only Those
who have Conquered it."*

THE CREED OF THE CONQUERING CHIEF.

Behold! I address this message to men of courage and ambition.

I bid you to fearlessly look upon the inner shrine wherein you hold dear your ambition of ambitions—that guarded secret which is nothing less than your desire to BE SUPERIOR—to be supreme in your life-sphere—to be dominant and TO LEAD.

In short—it is your *self* calling for CONQUEST.

I know my own heart in this respect. I know the fundamental traits of other men's hearts.

Unafraid, I express my self. I speak that which is within me. I talk of natural, inexorable laws. I set forth my own instinct. You will come to agree with much that I say.

If I advance opinions and tenets which surprise you—which you have never thought of before—which possibly "cut in"—then I ask you: *"Why should I be shackled by the cottony bands which most men allow to hold them in everlasting subjection? Why may I not dispel these gossamer threads of foolish tradition and maudlin sentiment which a mere breath of intellectual effort will scatter to the skies?"*

Go with me with an Open Mind, and the spirit of investigation; frankly admit that which you know exists and stand as a heart-deep law of your own hopes in this world.

I am to speak to you of the Creed of the Conquering Chief.

*1. From Philosophy, Nature and Science I shall draw lessons along this line, and deduct certain foundation principles. You will find that they combine into a code of Thought and Conduct which must characterize the person who is to actually demonstrate the idea contained in the title of this lecture.

It is not my intention to set forth views that will appeal to him "who runs and reads," but to him who *stops* and *thinks*.

Ponder well the thoughts that follow. Accept none that are diametrically opposed to your deepest beliefs —nor reject any merely upon sentiment, guess-work, or unwarranted prejudice. Test and weigh, apply and observe. If in your best judgment you can finally give it the stamp of approval—and by approval, I mean the decision that it is based upon Natural Law—then use as you choose.

There is nothing novel or new in the idea of Conquest. From the moment man first calls his vital powers into action in a gasp for breath at birth, on through the years until he again gasps for breath ere passing into the next state of being—he confronts the constant necessity of conquest.

It is instinctive and incessant.

*2. There are two major forces and impulses that forever spur on the activities of men. The sub-conscious mind cries "I Want"—and the conscious mind has an all-consuming desire "To-Be-Great." Achievement and Recognition are the twin Grails that man continually pursues throughout his crusade on this earth. He must obtain them or else he dies.

And chief of these is DESIRE TO BE GREAT.

"The desire To Be Great, is as dynamic a force in the human mind as the sun's rays to the growth of a plant. Because of its intensity, a man's mind machine drives only one way. It can stand any amount of success, and still strive for more, but it cannot long tolerate non-achievement and failure." So writes one of the apostles of the new psychology.

*3. It will be well, before going further, to have a clear understanding of the exact meaning of this subject. This will guard against needless misconception and bias. Note these definitions:

Creed:—A definite summary of what is believed; an exposition of important points, as in Science, Religion, Conduct.

Conquering:—The act of subduing or overcoming by Mental Power; to gain or obtain the Victory.

Chief:—A Commander; principal or most eminent in any quality or action; having the most influence.

Will you understand, then, that the "Creed of the Conquering Chief" is to be:

An investigation into the art of overcoming by Mental Power, and gaining the Great Victory through application of definite and important scientific lines of Human Conduct—resulting in the Commander; the person "eminent in exerting the most influence."

*4. We live in an artificial state of society. There is not the rugged, vital, aggressive type of man now, as of old. Members of the civilized social order are emasculated, as it were, if comparison is made with the *natural man*. We see foppery, vanity, and effeminacy on all sides. There is a fawning attitude, and a sinking of individuality.

There is a fading away of the steel and sinew which made the old-order grand type of leader. There is a rising up of organizations, combines, etc.; there is the "lodge" and "linked-together-for-mutual-protection" fraternal clans.

Everywhere is a lack of "I" and the strength-sapping dependence upon the "we."

Let a man openly stand out—vibrant and pulsating with egoism—boldly expressing a rugged, vital self-hood and a dominant self sufficiency—and what happens? Just this: the gaping, unreliant, unaggressive, conquered mass—the subdued Crowd—follow him with their terrier-yelping. They cannot rise to equal dominance.

*5. The price that every Conquering Chief must pay for prominence is the envy, the calumny, the attack by the hordes lower down. It calls for masterful brain and nerve and manner to stay there—at the forefront.

Few people can summons the stamina required for the perilous position of Leadership.

It is the high art of Conquest.

Can *you* master it?

*   *   *   *   *   *   *

*6. If you could silently, quietly, clearly, peer into the hearts of the said failures in life—if you could once learn the never-revealed sombre secret of men and women who merely serve as the back-ground mass of humanity—the dark wall which sets forth in added brilliance the splendor of the successful—THERE, in that closed chamber, would be read the Tale of FEAR—cringing, hesitating, shrinking, servile COWARDICE.

It is a tragedy.

For it's the story of bright hopes blasted—the record of things hoped for, but never gained.

It's the life history of a good soul seeking higher levels of power and unfoldment, but bound and shackled and scared by an ever present: *"Oh, I dare not."*

It's the chronicle of youth's fine faith in a golden future, filled with health, happiness and financial ease —all gradually dimmed and blotted and finally sunk into oblivion. All because the race struggle for supremacy requires MEN WHO DARE.

In other words—men who are fired with the spirit of The Conquering Chief.

There are FOUR stages through which you mentally pass in establishing firmly the mood or tendency for conquest. These steps are

1. I *wish* for Conquest.
2. I *desire* to conquer.
3. I am *resolved* upon conquest.
4. I *DEMAND* and *INSIST* that I become a conqueror.

*7. If you are to go on with me, you must have the Open Mind.

Tens of thousands grind out their grist of human grief, in a never-changing, never-widening, soul-stunting narrowness of mental vision.

The Open Mind is the precursor of Progress.

*8. To accept some of the foundation principles to be here set forth, you may have to cast aside some long cherished delusions. Understand, I say you *may* have to—of course if you do not hold these unscientific tenets, you cannot cast them forth.

*9. First of all I would have you understand what

the Scientific method of investigation is. I give it to
you in the words of a sound thinker.

"Pure Science has four main principles at its foundation—analysis, synthesis, imagination and absolute
elimination of opinion and Self. It is hard to tell
which of these four is most important, but one in
particular represents the sum total of the difference
between scientific and unscientific method. The average man, untrained in the scientific method of thinking
when he approaches a problem, allows himself to sway
and stagger under the influence of his opinion, prejudice, bias, habit and ignorance. Science on the other
hand, deals with nothing but facts, has no opinions,
admits no prejudice, eliminates personal habit, analyzes
to the smallest possible atom, deals in fact only, and
admits nothing as a fact unless it stands the test of
ice cold reasoning and logic."

Read that again. Get it well into your manner of
handling matters. Know clearly what this Scientific
method of thought is. The Conquering Chief must
refuse either to assume something that does not exist,
or to be blinded by bias—and thus be led to lines of
action which are not based upon EXISTING FACTS.

The foregoing master analysis of the scientific
method yields the first great principle:

**Resolve to be swayed neither by feeling, senti-
ment nor guesswork, but always seek to discover
the underlying LAW and act upon that.**

*10. Now, the Conquering Chief must realize that
there is a natural rule of action—a definite "cause"—
preceding every desired Result. *"Big men search for
the underlying law—and obey it. They think, then
act,"* says St. Elmo Lewis. One of the very first prin-

ciples in Natural Philosophy is, that there can be no effect produced, without there being a Cause (law) in back of it.

Therefore, always seek for the underlying Law or Cause or Starting Point if you would produce any desired Effect. If instead of merely reading what I say here, and passing it by—you will begin to USE this principle, you can achieve wonders.

It has a tremendous bearing in EVERY field of human endeavor.

*12. You know that if you turn a railroad switch a certain way, it will throw the oncoming express into a siding—and wreck it. You know that if you put your finger into the fire, it will be burned. You know that if you jump from a high building down to the pavement, your bones will be broken.

These are mechanical and physical laws.

They have always existed. Man gradually finds out what they are, and then uses as he chooses. The possibility of wireless telegraphy existed ten thousand years ago, as it does now. But man did not then know the law. He did not know how to initiate the required Cause.

*13. I want to have you consider then, the analogy of this rather uninteresting analysis of Cause and Effect, as it applies to the Creed of the Conquering Chief—to your success in general. Right at this moment you are confronted by problems which you want to solve to the best advantage to yourself.

You want Success. You want Ability. You want Money. You want Influence. You want Culture. You want a hundred and one things.

If you will begin at once to investigate, observe, test, analyze and endeavor to find out: *What is the Law*

that will yield the next result I want? You can *find*
that Law and by putting it into operation you will
secure the Effect you desire.

I cannot go into the details of using this Law in any
particular way you wish to use it; I can only give you
the *principle.* It is for you, in your own individual
way, to discover the details, and COMBINE THEM.

*14. Few grasp the idea that SUCCESS in any
venture—in health, in personal power, in financial
achievement, in SELF-CONTROL, in Love, among
men or nations, or LIFE AS A WHOLE—is a tech-
nological affair. It calls for constructive efforts, massing of forces, subtle strategy of a type similar in principle to that required for great engineering feats—
achieving colossal effects through Thought and Action.

Therefore—go where you can be quiet, by yourself.
Clearly, frankly, without deceiving yourself—see just
what problems and obstacles confront you. "To crush
an obstacle, there is need of a giant hammer, and the
more mass that can be given it and the greater force
put behind it, the more deadly will be the blow." This
law of physics, applied to Conquest, translates into
this: Reasoning, thinking, analyzing are forces which
smash the obstacles which block your way.

*15. Plot with yourself to WIN, to crush obstacles
—whether of personal weaknesses, opposition of others,
unexpected developments. Plan out what you must do
to GAIN YOUR GOAL. Carry in mind the "giant
hammer" and the "greater force behind it" and in
every possible way MASS YOUR UTMOST POWERS
to crush each obstacle that bars your way to what you
desire.

Go forward with just as definite, detailed, pre-
arranged a plan as Napoleon prepared a battle map

months ahead of the encounter. Most people drift—
and the fickle tide of fate ebbs and flows. One day is
the same as another to them so far as any definite
PLAN, strategy, attack upon fortune, power, fame
and SUCCESS.

Strategy, brain-work, thought, speed, decisiveness—
these are your chief weapons.

*16. Knowing the Scientific method of thinking,
and using Natural Law, are the first essentials, then,
of the man of superior qualities. But balancing these,
must be the ability to APPLY this method, or as we
term it—*you must have POWER,* and this subject I
will consider in a moment.

The small, narrow mind sees only close at hand—
immediate connections and results. The broad, philo-
sophic mind sees in the *far expanse* and remote results
relations, rewards, AS WELL AS CLOSE AT HAND.
Demand for yourself the broad-gauge view-point which
considers all human relations and achievement and eras
in the light of world-processes.

*17. Before the advent of steam railways, electric
transportation, flying machines and automobiles and
ocean greyhounds—the average man was familiar with
conditions only within 15 miles from where he lived.

Today men know a thousand miles and more.

Don't stay in the 15-mile type of Mind—demand the
thousand mile radius—*the Open Mind.*

* * * * * * *

*18. I assume you are listening to this lecture, be-
cause there's a spark in your breast which urges you
up the "ambition route," to a position of chieftainship.
You wouldn't bother to come here unless you were
interested in the Creed of the Conquering Chief.

Boldly do I proclaim that you have the opportunity

and the power to attain what you now want. And then, with greater and more brilliant wants, you have the power to gain them and so mount indefinitely.

*19. Understand: Great Men perform Great Deeds; Great Needs give birth to Great Men.

Great men are not a race-apart—an exceptional drop from the sea of life—shaken loose once in an era.

Great Men are little men INTENSIFIELD—EX-PANDED.

Just as a big bubble is a little one into which has been breath increased energy.

*19. As Ibsen says in "Human Quintessence": "If we take *qualities* as the point of departure (speaking of great men) we can discover, notwithstanding the enormous variations of talent—NO REAL DIFFER-ENCE BETWEEN EVERYDAY PEOPLE and GREAT MEN, but only dissimilarity in gradations and degree. The qualities which give such men their superiority over others are, in their roots, COMMON TO ALL HUMANITY. They are, in the main points, the same as those which have secured for the human being as a species, his privileged position in planetary life. But in the individual offshoots they bloom with rare intensity. They express themselves here in a clearer mentality or a mightier will or a more refined and complex feeling."

This is summed up by a keen writer, Bruce Lan-downe, who says: "Your real self—mind, soul or spirit —whatever you call it—is perfect and complete. It possesses all the possibilities and powers of any soul in the universe; it can overcome, climb out from under, any and every limitation of self."

*20. Grasp the FACT here: you have within *your* make-up, EVERY ONE of the qualities and traits which the great man has. The degree to which you develop and apply these forces is to a very great extent *one of your own choosing.*

*21. The Conquering Chief—the successful leader —the great man—is one who rises above the average. But he is not separated from the crowd by a yawning abyss.

You have the endowment. *To what degree will you raise it?*

*22. Remember, to falter, hesitate, and back down on your plans—to give up—to weaken and lazily quit, is to dissipate the conquest power within you.

Make great plans—but forever fight forward for their consummation. Make plans at first well within your power of accomplishment. Stick to them. Achieve them.

When you have risen a degree—view from aloft the incline up which you have come. It creates confidence. It develops power. It instills courage. It steels the sinews for greater effort. Then gradually brave steeper ascents—try the larger task. Go upwards. Dominate. CONQUER—until you reach and master the big things. Some day in your career you will assay the Grand Ascent—your Life's Ambition: your Crowning Achievement in Life. Up, up you go, with adequate ability, clear sight, sure steps, iron grip, unfailing energy.

For so do the World's Great rise.

*23. Emerson, in his clear, precise way, tells us:

"Life is a search for Power; and this is an element with which the earth is so saturated there is no chink or crevice in which it is not lodged—that no honest seeking goes unrewarded."

You should interpret his use of the word "Power"

as meaning an intangible force, influence, medium or *"something"* which man can control and make use of to attain his legitimate goals.

*24. It is here that I want to introduce another element of our Creed as follows:

All the Power you can ever use now exists potentially within you and awaits your intelligent mastery.

*25. You will get inspiration from this gem by William Ellery Channing:

POWER.

"The Passion for Power is one of the most universal. The child never exults and rejoices more, than when it becomes conscious of power by overcoming difficulties, or compassing new ends. Power is the chief element of all the commanding qualities of our nature. It enters into all of the higher virtues; it enters into intellectual eminence. It is power of thought and utterance which immortalizes the products of genius.

"There are various kinds of power which it is our duty to covet, accumulate and hold fast. First, there is an *inward* power, the most precious of all possessions; of power over ourselves, power to stand trial, to bear suffering, to front danger; power to follow our convictions, however resisted by menace or scorn; power of calm reliance in seasons of darkness and storm. Again there is power over *outward* things, the power by which the mind triumphs over matter, presses into service the subtilest and strongest elements, makes winds, fire and steam its ministers, rears the city, opens a path through the ocean, and makes the wilderness blossom as the rose. These forms of power, especially the first, are glorious distinctions of our race, nor can we prize them too highly."

*26. All day long—from early morning till late at night—through the hurly-burly of the morning hours, and the push and pull of the advancing day—even impressed upon your mind as you go to sleep and often aroused into activity during your dreams—*you are searching for Power.*

You want Power to Succeed; you want power to do and to dare; you want power to deal with others; you strive for power to rise above the commonplaces of life —to be a leader. For instinctive in every man is a great natural desire for supremacy—the working out of a deep-seated principle *"survival of the fittest."*

In order to be able to think and draw conclusions, it is necessary to *acknowledge that which exists.*

This is the difficult thing for the mass of men and women. It is so easy, so entrancing, so beautiful to let the mind roam off into the Elysian field of dreams, of idealism; to shut our eyes to that which actually exists—the conditions in which we are really placed. A man may shut himself in a closet and vow there's no such thing as sunshine. And yet it exists just the same.

And from this statement I want to draw another bearing upon our Creed as follows:

Realizing that throughout the world, among all individuals, there is a fundamental Will-to-be-Powerful, and admitting the existence of this desire for dominance, I shall aim to make my conduct befit this large calibre.

*27. Men are not equal—never have been—and so far as we can now determine—NEVER WILL BE. So long as ambition enters into the measure of a man, and free will exists,—there will be leaders—and followers. There will be the great, and the small. Socialisms, Utopias, and any other plan of making men equal —will never stand the test of time. If to-day you should place the same opportunity before two men who are equals, what will be the result? I will let Prof. Tyndall tell you:

"Suppose two men to be equals at night, and that one rises at six while the other sleeps until nine the next morning—what becomes of your levelling? Nature secures advance, not by the reduction of all to a common level, but by the encouragement and conservation of what is best."

*28. The great authority, James J. Bryce, writing on "Equality" said:

"There has never been in the world such a state of natural equality as many have dreamed of. . . . It is not law that creates inequality of property. It is, in the first instance, strength, physical or intellectual; that is to say *inequality is due to natural, not to artificial, causes.* . . . If ten men were to be started, on Monday morning, with equal property, and left to themselves for six days, no two would be found to have equal property on Saturday night, because in no two would the faculty of acquiring and the habit of spending be the same." . . . It is by the power of devising schemes and conducing large commercial or financial operations that the largest masses of property are accumulated in one hand."

By a strange coincidence, within a few hours after finding the above, I picked up a current magazine which had just reached my desk. In it I read:

J. P. Morgan, King.

"J. P. Morgan was a king. There are two kinds of

rulers of men. One kind is chosen by heredity or the ballot; the other kind by the same process of natural selection that holds in nature—the process by which the oak becomes tallest, a bull strongest, a bird swiftest.

*29. "Democracy is only an affair of equal *opportunities;* it can never be a levelling of abilities. To the end of the human drama we shall instinctively continue to put forth our kings.

"A king is a man with that secret, mysterious something in him that makes him a master and causes others to be glad to serve. * * * * The real rule of men will always be a theocracy, composed of men raised up by the nature of things to command."

As a matter of fact, Nature does not know such a thing as equality. She distributes unevenly genius, beauty, health, vigour, intelligence, and all the qualities which confer on their possessors a superiority over their fellows. * * Can we suppose that societies will ever succeed in establishing artificially the equality refused by Nature. (And they say "Nature is God manifesting.") Not only does Nature not know equality, but since the beginning of the ages she has always realized progress by means of successive differentiations—that is to say, *by increasing inequalities.* These alone could raise the obscure cell of the early geological periods to the superior beings whose inventions were to change the face of the earth.

*30. Out of this thought we may weave another section for our Creed:

Success and conquest comes only from each man's individual efforts wisely, swiftly, incessantly exerted. Permanent power cannot be acquired by any artificial plan of levelling men. Only as you

**hew closely to Nature's plan of encouraging that
which is best, can you reach supremacy.**

*31.   Gerald Stanley Lee wrote a great book.
It is called *"CROWDS—a Book for the Individual."*
I wish I might stop and write a book: *"INDI-
VIDUALS—A Book for the Crowd."*

*32.   Lee, in his book, weaves a mind-gripping story
of crowds—people in masses. He talks of their ambitions, their machines, their goals, their methods. He
deals with where they are going; how they are going;
what they are after; how they are trying to get it; and
how they are trying to express themselves.

But always as the "crowd," the mass, understand.

It is a sort of socialistic interweaving of men in bulk
—the ebb and flow of the multitude as they surge along
through life.

*33.   A crowd represents a levelling of men—a
pulling down of the dominant—a lowering of leaders.
Not that the masterful man has committed any crime
against the laws of created beings—but simply because
he is above the mass, do they seek to pull him down.
"If we cannot get up where you are, mayhap we can
pull you down to where we are" is the attitude of the
crowd.

In other words, the social leveller's ideal is the anni-
hilation of the every-where active and always-has-been-
active law of LEADERSHIP—survival of the superior.

*34.   Is the grand forest giant that towers above the
others by twenty or thirty feet, an unhealthy principle
in nature? Is it a blot upon the surrounding forest?
Is it an illustration of an unfair law?

*35.   Is the shining, quivering, energy-charged turf-
king, that out-distances all other blue-bloods, unhealthy
and against natural law? Does he represent Nature

turned against herself? This fine pacer with the swifter step, the better combination and opposition of muscle, and the evener use of energy—the superior balance of bone against bit—is it an illustration of any principle unfair to other horses?

*36. And yet the "crowd" would pull down the Leader. *"He is great; we are not great. We want him down with us."* THAT IS THE PRINCIPLE RAMPANT TODAY.

*37. Against it must act the Law of the Conquering Chief.

Le Bon, the great French student of the crowd says: "The crowd represents a formless, headless being which can do nothing, and will do nothing, without a master to lead it. * * Affirmation, contagion, repetition and prestige constitute the only means of persuading them. The multitude will admit anything; nothing is impossible in the eyes of the crowd."

Yet the crowd lacks plan or methodical power to accomplish what it credulously thinks possible. You must do your own thinking, judging, deciding by yourself; do your observing, watching, acting independent of the crowd.

"Democracy, from Plato's to our own times, has never been defended by the great thinkers," says Emile Faguet. "Almost all of the thinkers of the nineteenth century were not democrats."

*38. Capacity being the principal factor of progress, the capable of each class rise while the mediocre remain stationary or sink. What could laws do in the face of such inevitable necessities?

In vain do the incapable pretend that, representing number, they also represent force. Deprived of the superior brains by whose researches all workers profit, they would speedily sink into poverty and anarchy. The prosperity of millions of workers is due solely to a small number of superior brains.

"The greatest enemy of personality is the crowd. The crowd does not want valuable men; it wants only useful men" says Martin in "Behavior of Crowds."

*39. And so, instead of the development of Crowd, in bulk—rather would I raise up here and there, that individual who is endowed for supremacy—for leadership—for command. To be sure there are "natural" leaders who raise themselves. But, there are also other finely endowed souls who, if the plan is opened to them, MAKE QUICK STRIDES TO THE GOAL.

*40. Oh! I would write a book for the INDIVIDUAL—and scatter it broadcast through the Crowd. Let them ponder over it. Let them draw conclusions. Let the lessons work upon an individual here and another there in that motley gathering. There are a few sparks slumbering in breasts which await the touch of hidden ambition to fire them with an energy which would brook no resistance.

* * * * * * *

*41. *"The fundamental failure of humanity so far is self-assertion"* says a clear thinker. *"Everything in a social machine, if it is a machine that really works, is based upon the profound and special study of the individual."*

The Creed of the Conquering Chief is one phase of such a study.

*42. I believe in the intense culture of the individual.

The mammoth chrysanthemum is the result of cutting away from the plant all other buds and shoots, and flooding that whole plant's life-force into the one magnificent bloom.

As Herbert Spencer puts it "Thus nature seems to speak in a continued protest against uniformity, by a thousand analogies insisting upon the supreme importance of the individual."

*43. I believe in this as applied to the individual. I believe in eliminating all the surrounding clods and worthless material. If you wish to interpret me as saying the "side-tracking of the crowd that demonstrates that it will NOT grow"—all right.

I believe in the man who forges ahead of the mass.

I seek the high altitudes.

I claim the open road for the great soul that can conquer.

I believe in the forest king among men.

I do not believe in organization—as effected today.

I do not believe in allying one's powers with others—as individuals.

I do not believe in a labor unionism that would shackle individual power and effectiveness—that would kill off the opportunity for leadership. I abhor any clique of miscellaneous men who want life on a uniform level.

*44. My ideal is a picture of energy-charged youth, reaching for the stars: heart aflame, mind aglow, body aquiver.

Give me the open road, minus a yoke, that I may run to the limit of my endowments and my own inner willingness to conquer. Allow me to pay my own price for the jewel of power—and let me buy just as brilliant a gem as I am willing to exchange personal effort for.

*   *   *   *   *   *   *

*45. I want aheadness-of-the-crowd.

*46. The torches of past civilizations and races of men still stand high enough to cast a light forward to this day. These pillars that still rise high enough to tell of long dead ages are simply THE GREAT MEN OF THOSE ERAS. If the crowd had its way—its life record would be levelled so low, with its Conquering Chiefs pulled down, that the turning rim of the world would have long since blotted its history from our view.

*47. Begin to raise your own light aloft — high; force from your path the scum that clutters your feet as you progress—those who cannot and will not face upward.

It is the Law of Life — the principle upon which the forest king rises aloft.

Get out of the Crowd. Do this by fashioning your mind on a pattern that deliberately rises aloof from that crowd.

*48. This is the law of the Conquering Chief.

*　　*　　*　　*　　*　　*　　*

*49. Inasmuch as you are here listening to this lecture of your own free will and choice, I shall take the time to consider even at greater length, this crowd-principle.

The idea of Conquest in the personal realm—the Law of Leadership—also links with it the existence of the "mass," or multitude. Its opposite is the humdrum thousands: drifting, shifting, swayed and dominated followers.

*50. It infers that there is a man here and another there who rises to supremacy. Hence, in order to a fuller understanding for attaining your position of command, you must know some of the characteristics which typify the crowd-man. This is in order that you may escape the negative influences in your own life, as well as to apply positive influences when required.

Ibsen, thru one of his sturdy characters, Dr. Stockman, says: "What sort of truths are they that the majority usually supports? They are truths that are of such an advanced age that they are beginning to break up. * * They are the origin of the moral scurvy that is rampant in our communities. * * The most dangerous enemy of truth and freedom among us *is the compact majority.* The majority has might on its side unfortunately, but *right* it has never."

*51. The great analyst of the Crowd-man, Gustave Le Bon, says: *"Man, as a part of multitude, is a very different being from the same man as an isolated individual. His conscious individuality vanishes in the unconscious personality of the crowd. Among other characteristics of crowds, we must note their infinite credulity, and exaggerated sensibility, their short-sightedness and their incapacity to respond to the influence of reason."*

This is just a way of stating that you must stand alone if you are to conquer. Men in groups, lose individuality. They see from an exaggerated, narrow, unbalanced viewpoint. They can not or do not use deliberate reason before acting.

*52. Let a leader, charged with magnetism (the art of influence) stand before such a crowd, and throw out stirring sentiments, and over the gathering he spreads a psychological mantle which carries them off their feet; it freezes self-control, deadens judgment, benumbs reason. And this assertion applies whenever the actions urged be for good or for ill.

*53. All progress of the individual is a matter of *inner unfoldment.*

Life moves from within, outward. The germ or vitality is always at the center, not on the surface. The growth of the tree or the plant, of the animal or the fruit, is not that of adding on the outside, but a supply from the inside.

*54. The individual determines his own position in life, according to the amount of intelligent effort exerted. It is for this reason, that men NEVER WILL BE EQUAL, because there are those—*the majority*—who will not work to acquire this Inner Power.

You, then, must rank among the Great, or the mediocre.

*55. As Victor Hugo remarks: *"Mediocrity is in favor of him who annoys her the least and resembles her the most. Out of all the stones that pickaxe and calumny and diatribe and insult can tear away from the base of the great man, a pedestal is erected for the second rate man."*

The Conquering Chief must make one grand fight against mediocrity—that type of commonplace, self-satisfied, lazy attitude which expects to be taken in hand by "fortune" and raised aloft.

*   *   *   *   *   *   *

*56. The master tool with which great men work in this world is *Intellect.*

With that wonderful gift is carved and cunningly wrought and ingeniously constructed all that has marked man's steps across the pages of history. It has reared temples, created beautiful art, produced marvels mechanic.

Also, used in a different way, it has stampeded races into annihilating conflict.

This great tool the workman MAKES FOR HIMSELF.

There is the colossal fact which makes of your life an opportunity and of success a rare reward.

Man can make himself into whatever he chooses. The rough metal for this tool is man's at birth—he makes and molds and uses it as he chooses.

*57. The human brain is a more terrible weapon than the lion's paw. Man's mental machine drives him ahead through life, slowly and blunderingly, or swiftly and surely, according to the power and efficiency latent in the machine itself.

One of the present day psychologists puts this into definite form as follows:

1. All human achievement comes about through bodily activity.

2. All bodily activity is caused, controlled and directed by the mind.

3. The mind is the instrument you must employ for the accomplishment of any purpose.

*58. The great man is the man who makes himself out of anything he finds at hand. As Lee puts it: *"If success cannot do it, he makes failure do it. If he cannot make success express the greatness of the vision that is in him, he makes failure express it."*

But always does there go into his plan of action the stream of conquest—he lives and moves in a sea which floods his consciousness always with the belief: "I am the power of accomplishment."

"I will win."

"I demand conquest of myself."

*59. Listen to the philosopher Schopenhauer's stirring words, be-speaking self-reliance and refusal to be drawn down by weakness:

"What people commonly call 'Fate' is, as a general rule, nothing but their own stupid and foolish conduct. * * The most finished man of the world would be one who was never irresolute and never in a hurry.

"Life is one long battle; we have to fight at every step. * * It is a cowardly soul that shrinks or grows faint and despondent as soon as the storm begins to gather, or even when the first cloud appears on the horizon. Our motto should be *'No surrender'*. * * As long as the issue of any matter fraught with peril is still in doubt, and there is yet some possibility left that all may not come right, no one should ever tremble or think of anything but resistance."

*60. If you ask me: *"Who are the great men, and when and how do they emerge from the mass?"*—I will ask you to listen to Nietzsche:

"The great man—a man whom Nature has built up and invented in a grand style—What is such a man? *First*, in his general course of action, his consistency is so broad that owing to its very breadth it can be surveyed only with difficulty, and consequently misleads; he possesses the capacity of EXTENDING HIS WILL OVER GREAT STRETCHES OF LIFE, and of despising and rejecting all small things, whatever most beautiful and "divine" things of the world there may be among them. *Secondly*, he is *colder, harder, less cautious and more free from the fear of "public opinion."* If he is unable to *lead*, he walks alone; in his dealings with men his one aim is *to make* something out of them. His greatness consists in this: to *will* something great, together with the means thereto. * * * The object is to attain that enormous *energy of greatness* which can model the man of the future by means of discipline."

*61. The aim of the Conquering Chief must be the acquirement of that huge ability or energy, capable of putting forth such a preponderance of power from *within,* that he will not be swayed or influenced by the powers *external.*

There are still certain tremendous forces of Nature, such as the cyclone, the lightning's stroke, the earthquake, which man acknowledges master. But there are lesser forces over which he has made himself Chief.

*62. In this connection weighty warning is given by the great thinker Haddock who says:

"Personal life is a play between the powers *without,* and the powers *within* the central function of Will.

Personal Life ends in subjection to such external powers *or rises to mastery over them."*

And before analyzing this principle, I want to set down another essential to our Creed:

The pathway to Power calls for everlasting vigilance, to the end that your own natural weak tendencies may be overcome by never yielding to their solicitations.

*63. The history of the human race as we know it, is one long, unbroken record of man's struggle to rise to mastery over *external* powers.

Man has come up from the brute. From the study of the earth's various stages of formation, Science tells us that life on the planet runs back more than six thousand millions of years.

The slow progress of the past, and the uncertainty of the future, is picturesquely put by David **Orr** Edson in this passage:

"The corridor of evolution, thru which man has journeyed from the slime of First Things to this day, runs ever uphill. Its floor is beset with obstacles and

pitfalls, and fearful things lie in wait to pounce upon
the traveller—humanity.

"Before us that same corridor still stretches away,
no man knows whither, although the dreamer now and
again catches a half vision of what lies at its end. Its
course is forever upward, and the traveler who stum-
bles along it catches his feet in the same obstacles
and fights back the same enemies that beset those from
whom he received the torch of life.

"For it is only through battle that man has lifted
himself from the ooze of primeval things. The history
of the race is the history of unending warfare against
tremendous odds, with the victory that is to crown the
end of the journey still a long way off."

*64. When man first confronted his environment—
Nature—back there in the midnight of human history,
when the first faint trace of Mind (that which forever
impassably separates us from the realm of brute creation)—when the first faint streaks of gray were beginning to modify the hitherto black night of living
things—back there men still fought *like* beasts and
with beasts.

This was his initial striving to acquire domination
and conquest over external powers.

*65. The first ally was the club, the hurled rock,
and similar means of offense and defense.

*66. As the gray-black of human history's begin-
nings was assuming the delicate rose-tint of the dawn,
man was acquiring still more sway over external
powers. He constructed a place of habitation and
made weapons—*since self-protection is the first law of
created life.*

So the tale of triumph runs. Personal life has come
up through the ages, ever acquiring more control, and

extending the individual's reach to a widening sphere
of mastery. First it was over other creatures; then it
was the Elements; then it was travel and navigation—
the crossing of a continent—the sending of messages
with or without mechanical connections; the conquest
of the air, etc.

*67. And there is still another goal to be reached—
the sending of Thought from Mind to Mind, without
any intervening physical agent.

*68. The day when men fought like beasts has
gone. We live in the great Age of Mind—an era when
Mental Forces reign supreme. The great successes
to-day—the Conquering Chiefs—are the men of great
mind-power.

From this we may draw a brief rule for our Creed
as follows:

**Mind-power is to-day the sole measure of mas-
tery. Resolve that your own Brain shall be made
to work for you with all its might.**

*   *   *   *   *   *   *

*69. To achieve this result, requires a massing of
the mind's powers—concentration. It is the unbound-
ed fertility of the brain to create IDEAS.

What, then, is the secret of concentration of personal
powers for conquest. What is the secret of a richly
productive supply of ideas?

For concentration I answer you: Firstly, be per-
fectly clear about what you want to do, and secondly,
by the faculty of imagination, picture yourself doing
it. "The man who is going to act successfully is he
who can hold the whole task in his mind's eye and see
himself performing it. The clear picture means the
clear purpose."

"What is it that inspires us with confidence in a

man? What is the secret of command that made a corrupt House of Commons tremble like slaves beneath the flashing eye of the elder Pitt, and the presence of Napoleon to be considered equivalent to a reinforcement of forty thousand men?

"Nothing more nor less than the fact that these men conveyed the impression of absolute concentration of purpose; their minds never appeared to vacillate, but went straight forward to the goal.

"Captains of industry are made of this stuff."

THE POWER OF AN IDEA

*70. The Conquering Chief, from the day of the cave man's discovery of the sling as a weapon superior to his arm-hurled rock, up to the present-day giants of conquest—whether in war, finance, science, thought —have all progressed through the POWER OF AN IDEA.

Says someone: *"the most potent, powerful, revolutionizing thing in the world is AN IDEA."*

Idea is Power!

Ideas rule the world.

An idea built the Universe.

A single idea—the sudden flash of a thought— may be worth a million dollars, and one *trained* mind can be the sponsor of a momentous plan. In your brain are real "ideas of power" awaiting the miracle of birth.

One idea birthed America.

Edison had an idea—and gave man the incandescent light.

Carnegie's brain flashed an idea into steel—and it paid him multi-millions.

Woolworth had just a 5 and 10 cent idea—but the

stores he sprinkled over the country have made many fortunes.

Single ideas issuing from the recesses of gray matter have made men immortal.

Ideas are conceived in the brain cells, are nurtured in their depths, and pass on to the miracle of birth.

Enshrouded in them is the marvel of divine creation.

Wonderful mental fruits grow in the fertile fields of the master intellects of a race.

Rich, virile, power-fraught ideas fairly overflow as they rush forth from the man-type termed "genius."

*   *   *   *   *   *   *

*71.   *Your* brain, so Science says, has a possible capacity for producing *over three billion ideas.*

How many of this uncountable number of ideas, hidden in your thought-cells, are you bringing into living and breathing existence?

Are you creating forceful thoughts?

Do feasible ideas fairly flash from your brain as sparks leap the gap in a static electric machine?

Are they making you bigger and better and more powerful in your life's sphere?

72.   There are milions of thought-cells in the human brain which are never used. Each individual has capacities that are never realized: powers that are never unfolded.

Why?

Largely because of sheer laziness to delve into the treasure vaults of the mind.

Most men go from cradle to the grave, unaware of the vast "acres of diamonds" locked in their own brains. "What a tremendous power lies coiled in the mind of man!" says Emerson.

A century ago the world watched with bated breath

as a crowning example of the power of ideas held sway.

One small man toppled kings off their thrones and made over the Map of Europe to suit his whims.

Why?

Sharp and clear comes the answer.—

SIMPLY BECAUSE HE HAD AN IDEA.

*73. And when Napoleon applied his strategy—he stood towering above the crowd, a Super-man headed for world domination.

It was the "power of an idea".

That's all.

*　*　*　*　*　*　*

And so—every man who is making his mark—every leader of men—every captain of industry—every wizard of invention—yes, every living human being who is going two-rounds-at-a-time to dazzling heights on the ladder of success, is doing it—

HOW?

—solely by means of the IDEAS which he makes his own brain produce.

*74. What are you doing to open the way for the "three billion capacity" of your brain?

As a Conquering Chief you must learn where ideas are started, how to have more and better ideas. You must learn how your brain works. You must become skilled in getting greater values from it. You must learn how to get the power out of ideas.

"There is no limit to the capacity of the mind for holding ideas. An overloaded mind is an ill-arranged mind. * * It may confidently be affirmed that there is nobody whatever who is incapable of developing genius in the right direction, for genius is as natural to man as is the flower to the seed."

*75. The other day I read this: "All light is at some point condensed into flame; in the same way every epoch is condensed into man. The man having expired, the epoch is closed—God turns the page. These different periods, which we name epochs, have all their dominant points. What is that dominant point? Is it the head that wears a crown, or is it the head that bears a thought? Is it an aristocracy, or is it an *idea?*

*76. Answer this for yourself.

Do you see in which direction the power lies???

*77. It's the man WHO HAS AN IDEA—and a Brain to nurture it—AND THE SPIRIT OF CONQUEST TO PUT IT OVER.

*78. Life's pathway never runs on a level—it is an incline on which you are either climbing up or slipping down. What is the secret of the *art of always GOING UP,* rather than down? In "Thus Spake Zarathustra" I find this:

"And this secret spake Life herself unto me, 'Behold I am that *which must ever surpass itself.'*"

From which flashes out a broad declaration of conquest:

Always will I strive to be greater than I am. I must SURPASS MYSELF. In each successive act, test, encounter, thought, I will BE GREATER than in the one previous. I am what I am now; but in an hour I must be MORE than I am now. In everything must I exert MORE POWER TO SURPASS MYSELF.

*79. The spirit of the foregoing theme is well illustrated by Stewart Edward White in the "Blazed Trail" where he says:

"Of these men Thorpe demanded one thing—success. He never tried to ask of them anything he did not believe to be thoroughly possible; but he expected always that in some manner, by hook or crook, they would carry the affair through. No matter how good the excuse, it was never accepted. Accidents would happen, there as elsewhere; *a way to arrive in spite of them always exists, if only a man is willing to use his wits, unflagging energy and time.* Bad luck is a reality; but much of what is called bad luck is nothing but a want of careful foresight."

*80. Surpassing of *self* is the first aim; surpassing of *others* is the second. This is the substance of Emerson's *"Every man believes he has a greater possibility."* You draw a circle to the utmost of your ability to-day, but on the morrow, lo—you must still draw one *outside* of that. You must *surpass yourself.*

This is involved philosophy, bordering, perhaps, upon mysticism. But—STOP AND THINK!

*81. *"Whatever cannot obey itself is commanded"* says the great writer on "surpassing self." The failures in life are the men who could not or would not obey themselves; they became commanded by others. They could not hold to the course; they lost their grip. They did not do as they promised their own hearts they would do.

*82. They failed to surpass themselves.

For such is the nature of things—he who cannot obey himself, in an ever increasing degree—is commanded by others.

*83. The Conquering Chief MUST OBEY HIMSELF—if he is to command others.

*84. It is here that I would have you work into your plan of action this declaration:

From now on I vow I will try to act the part of a man TEN TIMES BIGGER THAN I AM NOW, for by so doing, I construct greater powers in my own brain which will actually build me into such a leader. I refuse to be confined by the shadowy walls which heretofore have cramped me into a narrow sphere. From this day forth the word "limit" is banished from my mind.

THE MINUTE BUILDERS.

*85. You and I are architects of the minutes.

We build ourselves every moment.

What you are this minute is the result of what you were building during the thousands of minutes that already have passed.

What you will be a minute from now depends upon what you are now, *plus* what you are mentally demanding that this present moment shall add. Every turn of the second hand, are you building yourself anew—are you changing, altering, revising, remaking, INCREASING?

*86. Just as surely as the pilot of a vessel deliberately moves his wheel one way, and swings the huge greyhound to the east—or moves it the other way and swings it toward the setting sun, and so pursues his course as he elects, and finally reaching his port if his steering has been correct—just so can you deliberately direct your own course toward any goal.

*87. I repeat: You are the product of minutes. Each minute is an opportunity to build—for growth, advance, gain, supremacy, CONQUEST.

It all rests with you.

Keep your eyes on the minutes.

The minute makes the man.

The Creed of the Conquest calls for the everlastingly aggressive, watchful mind, which reasons, plans and forges ahead as the moments pass.

*88. Stop a minute, in the quiet, and see the logic of this. In your own inner sanctum YOU know what you are building—or not building. YOU know whether you are increasing your power. YOU know if you are gradually shrinking smaller and smaller in the life scale. YOU know what effectiveness or lack of it is evident in your building plans.

There's no limit to your building possibilities, if you will persist. One of the surest principles in the material world is this: *Nature achieves the grandest results by the simplest means—the constant adding together of atoms.*

*89. A gigantic planet is but molecules assembled.

Your life, your power, your fortune, is the addition of minutes.

From this draw a law of Conquest.

In the eternal flow of moments, each one contains a measure of power and success which I CAN add to my store. I resolve that never will I be found unmindful of this principle of conquest. I will gather power from every living minute. Alertness and ACTION are the qualities which secure this value.

*90. Again we find the author of the "Blazed Trail" saying:

"It is a drama, a struggle, a battle. We are fighting always with Time. * * When we gain a day we have scored a victory; when the wilderness puts us back an hour, we have suffered defeat. *Our ammunition is Time;* our small shot the minutes, our heavy ordnance the hours."

⁂91. Be a Builder of Minutes.

"THE SPIRIT OF THE DAY"

⁂92. As a companion thought to the "minute build-ers," the Conquering Chief will find great help in practicing the "Spirit of the Day" plan here outlined, which I introduce by asking:

Do you want buoyancy for the day; do you want power; do you want zest and activity and personality and happy accomplishment of the day's tasks. Do you want a bit of strategy applied in the morning that will carry you successfully through the hurly burly of the day? Then learn to use the "Spirit of the Day" based upon the following:

Going to one's work in the morning is rarely done with mental preparation. The body is started allright by giving it a supply of food. The more important ally, the mind, is usually left to hit-or-miss conditions. Herein lies a *major cause* for lost motion, loss of time and accomplishment, lack of pleasure, waste of nervous forces, etc.

The "Spirit of the Day" is of tremendous importance and a few minutes given to its practice in the morning while preparing for the day's activities, will pay extraordinary dividends in accomplishment and happiness.

The idea is to make up your mind before you start out, what predominant state you wish to carry through the day with you. Shall it be Courage? Health, Energy? Feeling of power? Confidence? Rapid Thinking? Financial Skill? or what.

Determine each morning, WHAT the "spirit" is you wish to be uppermost for that day. Select a different quality each day. INTEND the mind to

build that quality all day long. And the mind *will
do it*.

The Conquering Chief says, before the day's duties
begin: "Today I CONQUER. I am strong, brilliant,
magnetic," etc.

*94. The story of man's conquest on this earth as
we read it in the records of the past, has an ever
recurring similarity. It repeats itself. Hordes of
men have trod earth's crust—and passed on. Civilizations have risen to great heights and now sleep in
silence.

Even we at this late day, with fifteen centuries
lapsed, can gaze back upon the life and action of one
of these great cycles—as we watch on history's screen
the Rise and Fall of the once-great Roman empire.
Prior to that numberless other nations have risen and
fallen.

We think we have invented wonderful things—have
learned rare Arts—have produced phenomenal results.
We have. And yet the musty, mystic symbols and
traces of ancient races tell us of slumbering peoples
that have known them "as of old."

*95. The sun rises and sets to-day. It has done this
for ages. And because of this fact we say IT WILL
CONTINUE TO DO SO. We say it is *an established
law*.

*   *   *   *   *   *   *

Very well, then, carry this principle in mind for I
will soon propound one of the central laws we are to
deduct in the Creed of the Conquering Chief.

*96. Men have come and gone—and their lives yield
certain laws which we must admit as *established*, and
ready *to produce the same results* whenever the same
or comparative conditions are present.

I shall now give you a sombre, stop-and-think statement. From one who (pursuing the scientific method of investigation) has cast personal bias, sentiment, and theory to the winds. He speaks solely from a master insight into the plan of action of Conquerors. If I could explain away or reject his assertion, gladly would I do so. But clearest, coldest reasoning seems to establish it as a FACT. And as a part of our creed bespeaks for the acceptance of *"established fact,"* I give to you as follows:

"Every one who would be FREE must show his power. Unalterable remains the basis of all earthly greatness. He who exalteth himself shall be exalted. Bravery includes every virtue; humility every crime."

And in this Age of Mind you must understand Bravery to mean MENTAL courage. From this rises another Creed axiom:—

Always positively assert your own mental superiority. Be not a worm of the dust nor a meek follower and yielder to others. With vigorous, clear, swift mentality boldly attack the problems confronting you. Remember that the main difference between the submerged millions and the towering leaders is largely one of Brave Self-assertion.

And again the shout of the grim philosopher cuts our hearing with this:

"Therefore, if you would conquer Wealth and Honor, Power and Fame, you must be practical and cool. Only the powerful can be free, and Power is non-moral."

*97. The strong man masses his combined energies —mental and physical, in an assault upon difficulties. He is calm, cool, concentrated, scientific, swift and sure—a living illustration of his best powers in action.

"There are three great links to the chain that holds the human mind a prisoner. Together they fix a limit upon the activity of human thought, but a limit, remember, *that varies extremely with the individual.*"

But get the point—IT VARIES.

First of these links is man's heritage from his past experience, his unconscious recollection of the experiences gathered in his upward climb from chaos. Hard and rigid is the link. Man of the present cannot alter what has happened to his forebears.

And this explains WHY the spirit of conquest is in the make-up of all mankind of the past—of the present—and will be of the future.

*98. At this point I wish to defend certain of my principles.

I realize that they are not exactly in line with so-called "brotherly love," "golden-rule-ism," etc.

*99. I say this: theological postulatings; theories, assumptions and "taken-for-granteds," based upon sentiment, upon "heart-work," are one thing. Scientific data based upon existing facts is another. Once in a while a man is willing to talk along the lines of cold-blooded, unsentimental, uncolored reasoning: set solid upon established fact—worked out with deliberate analysis.

*100. Philosophy, as a phase of religious exposition, has dealt largely (speaking by illustration) with the golden hues of the fruit; with the emotions awakened by the soulful music. But Science has come along and cut the apple open and dealt with the real heart of the matter—it has considered the seeds that are to grow other apples. Likewise, instead of considering only the rich harmonies of the music—it has found out how many vibrations per second in the ether will cause these tones.

*101. Philosophy deals with "heart-stuff."
Science deals with cold fact.

*102. And so I say: The idea of individual supremacy and conquest—this thought of personal triumph, and the principle of rising above others—is just the illustration of a huge law of nature—*the survival of the fittest.*

This is evident in all branches of the living world.

*103. The philosopher Edmund Shaftesbury writes to the point on this subject:

"As civilization cannot ascend the plane of progress to its higher realms except under the law of the survival of the fittest, only those men and women who are fittest are desirable citizens of the earth; and they alone are welcome guests of Nature.

"All progress has taken place over the dead bodies of earth's millions. Humanity has been an unconscious sacrifice at the altar of change. But the change has been for something always growing better. With an iron hand nature has lead the march, and with a relentless dagger she has cut her way through the weaklings of the world.

"She has ordained that the fittest shall survive, and the fittest have always been the best fighters (Conquering Chiefs). She never thought of anything other than war and conflict, enmities and combat, in settling the question of supremacy.

"It is useless to argue that she has changed her plan. Her weapons are more active than before; that is the only difference. * * Nature has no use for weaklings. She abhors them, and never pities them.

She treats them in the most cruel manner. Humanity did not make nature and has no control over her purposes. We are all held under her sway in countless ways."

The virtue of the foregoing for you — a "Conquering Chief" is in the *principle* which it explains. This principle you adapt to your pursuit of power, health, success, fortune building; mental unfoldment.

*104. "But," say the heart-influenced teachers of philosophy and ethics: "The reason that conquest and survival of the fittest should not be followed as a principle, when we reach the heights of the human mind, is because that grand possession "soul," separates mankind from the lower orders and warns him to overlook the action of such a law."

All right then! They say because man has "soul," he comes in another class from all other living animals.

*105. Well, what is this so-called "soul," then, which is claimed as the dividing line between natural animals which do live out the law of conquest, and the animal man—which is supposed not to exemplify it?

The "teachers" will reply: *"it is the imperishable part of the human person—it is the man "himself"— his spark from the Divine Fire—his drop from the ocean of Infinite Life"*—and that sort of thing.

Allright, again; admit this to be true.

*106. Then follow this thought: Science, working upon its hard and fast, sentiment-minus basis—swayed neither by emotion nor personal opinion, says and proves the following: *the first forms of organized life on this planet run back to a form of shell fish in the slimy ooze of a Devonic age a million years ago.*

*107. Gradually, as the centuries flung their quick

years into the background of eternity, this starting point of life began to evolve a more complex form. It passes from the shell-form, to that of the vertebrae (having a backbone—the first foundation for Conquest-power, as it were). Then, as the centuries come and go, it develops the four-footed animals and reaches the lower forms of man-shaped animals.

Suddenly (not in the sense of a quick change so far as time-period is concerned, but as contrasted with the old order of animals) a leap forward is made—and there stands on the earth, prehistoric man.

*108. This is millions of years backward from our day. Again a jump forward, immeasurable compared with the old forms—and there begins that wonderful era on this earth—the so-called "Third Great Year." It is here there enters recorded history the first Dynasty of the Human Race—our first definite traces of man *as a man.*

*109. Now see this: from the shell life of millions of years ago, through all these tedious stages of progression and evolution—on up through to the man-giant of today: WHERE IS THE DIVIDING LINE? At what point does "soul" come into evidence? At what period does the animal soul transform into "man soul"?

*110. This idea of "soul" is something that is said-to-be; something assumed and allowed. But it is not now, nor has it ever been, broken open and analyzed and its make-up shown in concrete terms. Science cannot help us here, for the soul cannot be found to be analyzed in a matter-of-fact way.

*111. Well, what I am getting at by means of this digression is this: since we do not show where the dividing line stands between animal and man in this

"soul" region—and as objection to using the Law of
Conquest and the survival of the fittest has been based
upon the assumption of man being above such a law,
because he has a soul—then I insist upon classifying
man as an animal on this earth's crust, and that so far
as his relation to others of his kind, he is in the struggle for existence and he will fight for supremacy and
conquest—regardless of "soul science."

So I present the bold declaration that:

"**Those of earth who pretend to disbelieve in
rulership, and control, must learn that the first basis
of life is order and supreme mastery. You will
never find that a law that prevails in the sky, con-
tradicted by nature on earth.**"

*112. Understand this fact: philosophy, ethics,
religions, sects, clans, groups, juggle with many great
ideas which are based upon *assumptions*. To illus-
trate: a few of us conceive the idea that we wish to
influence a mass of men to act in a certain way
(naturally, for our own profit). So we get together—
the few of us—and we say: "*Assuming* this and that
to be true (whether or not incontrovertible Science
will prove it to be so)—why then, mercy upon us!—
all these other codes, which we have worked out,
BASED UPON THE ORIGINAL *ASSUMED* PRIN-
CIPLES, must be plain as day."

"Now, we'll just arrange our 'net results,' drawn in
from the original assumed belief, into a code. Of
course the mass must accept it, for it is logical when
tested against our 'first principles' which we started
with."

*　　*　　*　　*　　*　　*　　*

*113. These "first principles" might, or might not
be true. As I said, they were "assumed" at the start

without proof. Hence it is impossible to call them scientific (that is, demonstrable in a true-to-fact way).

*114. Now, after a time—after the original creators of this *assumed code* have passed along—and generations have accepted these rules of conduct—have taken them and lived according to them, merely upon the say-so of their forefathers—then it becomes a well-nigh universal belief that such a code is *exact.* And the believers call it the height of absurdity, hypocrisy, presumption and audacity *to in any way question the rules of the code.*

"Deprived of all constructive power, the theorists of all ages have always been very ready to destroy. Napoleon at St. Helena stated that 'if there existed a monarchy of granite the idealists and theorists would manage to reduce it to powder'."

*115. I go into this at such length in order to suggest to you that we are today swayed and led by religious beliefs, political tenets, and social conventions which MAY be the outworking of ASSUMPTIONS of centuries ago.

*116. Therefore I say: do not be afraid to question any established code of conduct. It may be right. It may be wrong. And I bring this axiom forward to you:

Leadership in so far as possible, progresses on KNOWN and SCIENTIFICALLY ESTABLISHED principles.

"Take nothing for granted" is a rule of peculiar significance.

*117. Perhaps you say: *"It is instinctive to cling to these faiths."* You may say: *"Involuntarily and unsought they rise up from somewheres in man's being."*

Let's analyze this "instinct" which you say repels you from the use of the Creed of Conquest.

*118.   Man of today has plenty of "instincts" which have been stamped into his make-up during the progress of the race.   We have instincts which did not appear until ages after the first appearance of the race upon the earth's surface.

*119.   It is possible for one man, or a body of men, to instill new "instincts" into a yielding and thoughtless and dassent-think-for-themselves following.   Inner moving motives can be germinated, and nurtured and brought forth in men's minds without their knowing it.

Under the sway of mental domination (the secret by which vast numbers of men have been led and moved to action)—a strong mind bearing over, influentially, upon a weaker one—an exerting of authority upon weakness and ignorance—I say upon this basis, a crafty class of preposterous prophets have led hundreds of thousands into the acceptance of certain beliefs which should be discarded as mental refuse.

*120.   Those so led believe they are following *natural instincts*.

Let a man with a live mind and the spirit of conquest consider these absurd faiths and he will reject them with the utmost scorn.

Yet these rules have for so long been ground into the sinew and fibre of the people that they call them "instincts."   They are by man originated, by man impelled, and by man maintained.

*121.   And believe me — *no man ever created an instinct*.

The individual blindly adhering to these witcheries of the soul is helpless before a keen intellect that questions them, and tears them apart and exposes the sham upon which they are built.

Learn to use the art of Interrogation. Ask questions. A keen business writer of our day says "The Power of the question is terrific." Ask questions long enough and keen enough and any problem within man's power can be solved.

*122. So I beseech you: do not softly sit down and quietly accept as "holiest truth," all that masquerades under the garb of "Instincts" divine laws and similar sham.

Understand me clearly—I did not say not to accept *anything* that is so classed; I said not to accept *ALL,* that is so termed.

*123. And from this emerges one of our main codes which is arranged as follows:

1. The Great Intelligence of the Universe, revealing through Nature, never advances on theories, sentiments, feeling, guesswork, or on any basis excepting that of Unalterable Law.

2. All unsound reasoning, wishing, hoping of man is swept aside and counted as naught before the unchangeable LAW and FACT of Nature.

3. Nature asserts — and infallibly demonstrates— that the man who leads and succeeds and takes the richest prizes, must be calm, cool, confident and COURAGEOUS.

4. The "survival of the fittest" is the deepest, soundest, most clearly evident LAW of Nature relating to the coming and going of life on this planet.

5. Nature, with an object in view—a result to be accomplished — never hesitates, dawdles or delays. Neither does she ask permission to per-

form, but strikes out boldly and intrepidly, STRAIGHT FOR THE FINAL GOAL.

*124. With the foregoing in mind, I have observed that men can be divided into three main classes:

1. The men of *Will-power* (the leaders).

2. The men of *Desire* (those whose intentions are good but who fail to put forth the necessary Dominance and Action to win out. They are the men who "wish" instead of DEMAND).

3. The men of *Fate* (those who give up all the glory of human achievement because they say *"it's all no use — things will never come my way."* This remark is correct: they certainly will never "come" but they can be APPROPRIATED—and that is what the Men of Will-power do).

*125. The Conquering Chief naturally belongs to the first class—the dynamic personality *asserting* its own; *claiming* its own; and invariably striving to make ACTION of the particular character required to *win* its own.

*126. Look to the biography of the world's great men, living or dead, and in nearly every instance one masterful trait stands out more prominent than all others. It is the real *secret* of their supremacy. And this I term indomitable, unconquerable WILL—self-declared refusal to yield an inch to the external forces which seek to thwart progress.

Napoleon was a superlative example of it; Bismark had it; Grant illustrated it splendidly; Morgan mastered it; Roosevelt in action was a whirlwind example of it; Edison owes his famous concentration and persistence to it. Yes—the captains of Industry, Finance,

Invention, Art, Science—all build their immortal achievements upon invincible Power of Will.

*127. " '*I will*' is the Sovereign state of Mind—the most intense attitude of Self towards all external forces. Your *Self* with *Will* in action has for servants the Body, Intellect and the Feelings. And with these servants fully disciplined, the sovereign Self goes forth to conquer a World, a Universe."

And for this reason, I would play up strong, in bold-faced type:

Knowing that only as I enter the ranks of the First Grade of men—THOSE OF WILL POWER —can I expect to be a Conquering Chief, I do pledge myself to the large development of this Prime Quality. I will neither passively wish for things, nor drop back to the third grade of those who abdicate their realms under the delusion that Life is a matter of pre-arranged destiny.

It is around this central power of WILL that the whole contest of conquest revolves.

*128. Every great Nation—living or dead—has come up to power by means of conquest. Every great nation and race to-day maintains its independence because of the inherent ability to conquer—to maintain its freedom. When nations attack, the strong, the skillful, the scientific become victors.

Now, this same law or principle acts among the individuals who collectively make up such a nation. The analogy holds good; it extends from the nation to the individual. Skill, strength, science (ALL AS PHASES OF MENTAL POWER)—maintain sway to-day.

* * * * * * *

*129. I suggest to you that there are two compo-

nent elements of Conquest. Namely: Strategy and
Weight. In the human individual this translates into
Plan of Thought plus *Energy in Action*. The two
multiply into each other, though always does one
degree of Strategy accomplish as much as two degrees
of Energy. Strategy is the superior quality.

*130. Conquest is—certainly is most likely to be—
the crowning result of concentrated energy. Conquest
—the "science" of conquest is the science of energy—
is Energetics. No sooner have we found this, the true
name of the study of Conquest, than we at once see
that we are dealing not with a vague, unaccountable,
unbalanced series of chances, but with a force which
by its very intensity excludes absolute irregularity.

The intenser a force the more will its line of movement approach to a straight line. If Energy is anything, it is intense, being intense, it is more apt to be
regular, rhythmic, measurable.

*131. Energetics is the study not of personal forces
generally, but of strategic personal forces.

Strategy, brain work, speed, decisiveness, knowledge
of vital facts—these are your chief weapons for conquest.

The writer, Morgan, says of Napoleon Bonaparte:

"At the end of a bloody half day struggle, there
came the inevitable hour of weariness and irresolution
for which Napoleon always waited and watched the
ebb and flow of the battle tide. Then he called out
'Eighty guns, Druot'. The guns, being quickly parked,
opened their mouths and poured forth a torrent of
iron and fire which tore through the enemy's line and
put them to flight. War was a terribly simple thing
with Napoleon."

The Conquering Chief—you—in dealing with others

must adapt this principle. In contests of wits, brains, plans, persistence, STRATEGY, watch for the moment when a stalemate seems evident; when the opponent rests in the lull of the struggle. Then summons swift, driving reserve powers—your second-wind powers of nerve and brain—your whole person massed—*and force the issue as you want it.*

I declare to you: for the man who peers beneath the surface—CONQUEST, too, is a "terribly simple thing."

*133. Concentration is the other element of Conquest. To a great general a war is not a series of sparring matches. On the contrary, he goes into every battle with the purpose of fighting to a finish, and he means to end the war with one staggering blow over the heart of his foe.

You must make every encounter, every new deal, every plan, every idea, every desire for greater success —greater power—greater wealth—the concentratd, all-absorbing thought and aim for the time being. Bring every legitimate force you can command into the fray. Strike the heaviest possible blows against the obstacles, and constantly hold in mind the unbeatable resolution to FIGHT IT OUT TO A SUCCESSFUL FINISH.

That's the trouble with most people—they do not use the conquest principle of "fighting to a finish."

*134. And I have given you the foregoing because it is very important in the development of the Conquering Chief that you understand this analogy.

There is a delightful passage in the old Norse Sagas which I want to bring in here:

"When Svipdag came to the gates of the burg, they were closed (for it was customary to ask permission to see, or take part in the war games). BUT Svipdag

did not take this trouble. He BROKE THE GATES
DOWN and rode in.

"Queen Yisa said, '*This man will be welcome*'."

From this you may draw this law:

Ask of no man permission to perform that which
is within you to do. Boldly strike out upon your
own initiative, and DO while the multitude stand
by in mouth-stretched awe. The reliant, the bold—
the Conquering Chief steps forward and plucks the
prize while others marvel at his daring.

*135. In what has thus far been written I have
given you underlying principles. Grim and sombre
and opposed to ordinary teachings perhaps, but nevertheless the BED ROCK of leadership up to the present
moment in man's history. And so far as we know—
to be the bed rock in the future.

*136. Understand—I am not writing to mental
weaklings, nor to dare-not-look-facts-in-the-face dream-
ers. It is a matter of interest to Thinkers WHO CAN
LOOK TRUTHS STRAIGHT IN THE EYE. And
the definition of truth is "*that which is, has been, or
will be.*" These things HAVE BEEN, ARE NOW,
and so must be accepted as Truths.

It is here that I wish to introduce something of a
lighter and more inspirational nature. For long I
have wanted to give you the following, which I term:

THE FOURTEEN ELEMENTS OF
PRACTICAL POWER

1. ENERGY is inherent power.

Cultivated as follows: You are invited to suppose
yourself about to undertake some enormous physical
and mental task. Are you ready? Summon, now, all
the energy of your being. Do not move a muscle.

Attend to the sense of *energy*, all over the body, or concentrated in the mind. Now for the task! You are equal to it! It shall be done! Control. Do nothing * * * * * * You have caught the idea of the *energy* sense. Practice it until that sense is ever at your instant command.

2. FORCE is active power.

Developed by multiplying self into every department of the business.

3. FIRMNESS is controlled applied power.

Put the idea of the strong, even hand-grasp on a weapon or tool into the handling of people and situations.

4. INDEPENDENCE is superiority over foreign power.

Developed only by deliberate, persistent growth of such consciousness and by conduct free from dependence.

5. SELF-RELIANCE is confidence in personal power.

Grown by openness of opinion coupled with valuation of one's own judgment.

6. RESOLUTION is courage-power and confidence-power united.

It is unfolded by the incessant mental affirmation: *"I can and I will, and the thing shall be done."*

7. DETERMINATION is power applied and held.

Cultivated by doing all sorts of things clear to the end, whether important or no, every day for months.

8. DECISION is power promptly applied.

Acquired by exercise and quick observation and swift deliberation and forced choice, *followed by instant action.*

9. PERSISTENCE is continuing power.

Attained by bringing to best finish every detail, no matter how trivial.

10. ENDURANCE is resisting power.

Brought about by declining, with great energy, to yield to contrary solicitation.

11. DARING is power loosed in full.

Cultured by letting go full physical power, by throwing self resolutely into certain kinds of action concerning which you are fearful or nervous, and by contact with daring men and situations, and by brave thought concerning big ventures.

12. PUSH is overcoming power.

Secured by the habitual energetic thrusting forward of self and business.

13. RESTRAINT is power balanced by power.

Cultivated by attending to reasons for caution and self control.

14. TACT-WILL-POWER is personal ability nicely adjusted to other wills for the sake of pleasing and winning.

It is all the above powers FINESSED IN ACTION.

You cannot study the foregoing analysis too often. Especially the bold face definitions should be memorized and frequently recalled and throughout the day constant effort made to make ACTION correspond.

*   *   *   *   *   *   *

*138. May I introduce to you one of the little known Laws of Conquest? I found it in the writings of Henri Bergson.

"The first impulse is to seek shelter; the second, which is the better, is to become supple as possible for flight *and above all for attack*—attack being the most effective means of defense.

* * And in a general way, in the evolution of life, just as in the evolution of human societies *and of individual destinies* THE GREATEST SUCCESSES HAVE BEEN FOR THOSE WHO HAVE ACCEPTED THE HEAVIEST RISKS."

*139. *"The greatest successes have been for those who have accepted the heaviest risks."* Mull over that for some time. It's the "whole thing" to the Conquering Chief. The daring to reach for the biggest attainable prizes—before which the multitude stand in awe—this is a central law.

*140. "Is the swallow, accustomed to fly upwards and enjoy the sunshine, born to live with the mole in darkness?" asks Eugene Sue.

Do you have the burning desire to soar above the hum drum crowd—to break from the shackles of convention—from the narrow traditions of the thought-bound?

Are you going to do it, or stay submerged with the mole in darkness? The swallow—mere bird—refuses to do it. Why should YOU—man or woman—remain in the depths!

*141. The world is filled with cowards who dare not attempt big things. Convention, and ridicule and "what will people say?" are ghosts which take the starch from them. Forget these bugaboos. Kick 'em into the scrap heap. The best successes are open to you if only you take the heaviest risks—ever balanced by cool, discerning judgment.

*142. *"Dare what no other man will dare. Seek to accomplish what no other man would attempt, is the very way to display yourself as a superior being in your own and in others' eyes."* Every phenomenal conquest but testifies to the abandoning of tradition in the man's inner mind. It is sheer decisive, dazzling DARING that wins out for scores of big men of the present day, and the gaping onlookers haven't the faintest idea of the real truth of the matter.

*143.   Danton, addressing the French revolutionists said: *"In order to defeat the enemies of this country we need audacity and still more audacity, and always audacity ! ! !*

In the "Psychology of Revolution" I found this gem:

"The revolutionary audacity which results in discoveries, implies very rare faculties. It necessitates notably an independence of mind sufficient to escape from the influence of current opinions, and a judgment that can grasp, under superficial analogies, *the hidden realities*. This form of revolutionary spirit is creative."

Take your "cue" from that.

*   *   *   *   *   *   *

*144.   Oh; I confess I am not advancing a philosophy and creed for the mass (considered as a mass). Here and there is a man who will gather together the threads of this lecture and weave for himself a wonderful fabric.

I believe in that individual.

I believe he is coming to supremacy.

I believe in the man who works out his own destiny on a grand scale.

But I do not believe in the man who leans—who cannot stand alone.

My idea of strength is the rugged oak on the mountain peak. Stalwart and sturdy; growing and existing against the odds of nature.

*145.   The price for this prominence among men is

the struggle to tower above belittlement, insult, jeer, sarcasm and insolence.

Can *you* pay that price?

Will you pay that price?

*146. Listen to this, then:

"Little by little, as the twilight of ancient things was approaching, a sufficient shadow was created around the monarchy for the sombre splendor, peculiar to great men of revolutions, to become visible to the eye. MIRABEAU WAS BEGINNING TO RADIATE."

*147. There is one of the fine "inspiration-stimulators" of modern literature. May you feel the thrill and upward urge of that passage. May you see in your mind's eye all the thought it holds—the sombre background, the brilliant central figure RADIATING POWER. A genuine CONQUERING CHIEF.

*148. Here highly resolve that you too will begin to Radiate—against a background of the ever-present commonplaces in life. Build you a structure of personality and achievement that will stand out in bold, rugged, bright outline against the twilight sky.

Be a Conquering Chief.

* * * * * * *

*149. Oh! I ask you: *"What is life worth if it be not filled with a wonderful effort toward great accomplishment?"*

*150. The business philosopher Louis Balsam, writing on the subject of "Self-Made Slaves," said:

"We have such strange, little, craving bodies, capable of such stupendous joys, such magnificent expression—and of such dreary, monotonous, fear-governed routine. How wistfully each of us regards the other and how fervent is our envy of those who seem to have happiness. Dimly troubled by the stirrings of our own possibilities, we go along inhibited by our dismal, unnecessary, but thoroughly human fears.

"The possibilities of life are bounded only by the skies. Everywhere about us, if we listen carefully, is movement and vibration that is in lyric rhythm with the motion of the universe. Rich, beyond the dizzied dreams of mankind, in opportunities for a bigger, fuller, more creative and joyous existence, life beckons us alluringly."

*151. What is a man's frame and vesture worth as a home for his soul and intellect, if his veins are not filled with a fire and an energy that give no peace when lazy loafing seeks to lull him to sleep?

Grant me the right to a life of strife and attainment.

*152. As was said of a real Conquering Chief:— "He delighted to hurry through his dominions, to multiply himself by rapid movements, to gather at a glance the capacities for improvement which every place possessed; to suggest plans which would startle by their originality and vastness; to project in an instant, works which a lifetime could scarcely accomplish, but which would leave behind the impression of superhuman energy."

*   *   *   *   *   *   *

*153. Refuse the dead stare of standing still—of accepting as final anything whatsoever. Man has erred for ages—we have found supposed truths to be errors. One device is succeeded by a better. Creeds and religions arise—and then better ones are born. Things of today will change—so will those of to-morrow.

The whole progress of man attests to the glory and grandeur of agitation—the desire for constant conquest and change—and for success rising to higher levels. "To augment, to increase, to win strength, to march forward, to be worth more today than yesterday —that is at once glory and life" says the philosopher.

*154. It is said that in Athens every man represented himself. Be your own representative and *make good to the last ounce of energy possessed.*

Constant, preparing Napoleon's wardrobe, for his meeting the Russian Emperor Alexander, remarked:

"Sire, your majesty desired to put on the large Russian decoration.

"Ah, it is true," said Napoleon, "come, put it on."

Then turning to Talma, the great actor who was present, he said "You see, we monarchs pursue the same course you do. We put on different costumes, according to the part we play. I wore a fez in Egypt, and today I put on the imperial star of Russia."

"But sire, everywhere you play your part *with masterly skill,* and the world, which is your audience, applauds your majesty" replied Talma.

*155. That is YOUR part.

PLAY WITH MASTERLY SKILL EVERY ACT. PLAY FOR THE CHIEF GOALS YOU SEEK. PLAY WITH YOUR MIND CLEAR AND OUR EYE OPEN. PLAY WITH THE CONSCIOUSNESS OF POWER AND ABILITY AND ABUNDANT ENERGY FOR WINNING WHAT YOU WANT.

*156. In time you are sure to create a stress in the nature of things, which must—not may, but simply *MUST* give way and open to you the road to Chieftainship.

And the Thought to hold is the Spirit of Conquest. It is the fire in youth's veins which attempts the impossible and presses forward toward the Infinite. Catch this thrill of conquest—fight on—admit into your mind no sense of limitation.

*157. What do you want most in life RIGHT NOW? Is it Money, Personal Influence, Social Recognition, Brain Power. Lay a strategic plan leading to what you want. Put the weight of your ENTIRE BEING—the white hot flame of intense desire—the WILLINGNESS TO PAY THE PRICE in intelligent effort into your spirit of Conquest—and it is won!

*158. I know what I say. I have experienced this thing—with blood rushing through my veins; with energies unexplainably multiplied; with nerves atingle with a sensation as though charged with vitality unmeasurable; with brain tensed and aroused to a rare readiness for creative thinking—thoughts flashing out over the whole world and experiencing a sense of touching the realm of genius. My eyes were opened to big financial vision and a courage-confidence for startling phases of practical ability awaited my command.

In short—it was a sure grip upon the Art of Conquest.

*159. The Conquering Chief may well read and review and ponder a lesson which I am to draw from that master study of fiction and fact "TOILERS OF THE SEA." Out in the ocean, on three barren rocks, the character "Gillatt" has essayed to recover single-handed the engine of a wrecked steamer. Just at the moment of victory, when about to sail his sloop home, a late summer equinoctial storm breaks forth in all its fury of wind, lightning and rain.

The huge endowment of conquest-power scintillates as the following depicts man's defiant, daring, and decisive battle against the elements in their worst frenzy:

"Gillatt was surveying the heavens in his turn. He raised his head defiantly now. After every stroke of his axe he stood erect and gazed upward, almost haughtily. He was, or seemed to be, too near destruction not to feel self-sustained. Would he yield to despair! No! In the presence of the wildest fury of ocean he was watchful as well as bold. He planted his feet only where the wreck was firm. He ventured his life, and yet was careful; for his determination, too, had reached its highest point. His strength had grown ten-fold greater. He had become excited by his own trepidity. The strokes of his axe were like blows of defiance. He seemed to have gained in directness what the tempest had lost. A pathetic struggle! On the one hand indefatigable will; on the other, inexhaustible power. It was a contest with the elements for the prize at his feet. The clouds took the shape of Gorgon masks in the immensity of the heavens; every possible form of terror appeared; the rain came from the sea, the surf from the cloud; phantoms of the wind bent down; meteoric faces revealed themselves and were again eclipsed, leaving the darkness still more intense; then nothing was visible but the torrents raging on all sides—a boiling sea; cumuli heavy with hail, ashen hued, ragged edged, seemed seized with a sort of whirling frenzy; strange rattlings filled the air; the inverse currents of electricity observed by Volta darted their sudden flashes from cloud to cloud. The prolongation of the lightning was terrible; the flashes passed close to Gillatt. The very ocean seemed appalled. Gillatt moved to and fro on the tottering wreck, though the deck trembled under his feet, striking, cutting, hacking with the axe in his hand, his features pallid in the gleam of the lightning, his long hair streaming, his feet naked, his face covered with the foam of the sea, but still grand amid the wild tumult of the storm.

But there was unquenchable fire in his eye.

Superb fire, will-power made visible! Such is the eye of man. The eyeball tells how much of the man there is in us. We reveal ourselves by the light under our eyebrows. Petty consciences wink; grand consciences flash. If there is no spark in the eyeball, there is no thought in the brain, no love in the heart. He who loves, wills; and he who wills, lightens and flashes. Resolution gives fire to the look—a fire composed of the combustion of timid thoughts.

The headstrong are really the sublime. The man who is only brave owes it to impulse; the man who is only valiant merely possesses that temperament; the man who is courageous has only one virtue; the man who is headstrong in the truth is sublime. All the secrets of great souls lie in the one word *Perseverando*. Perseverance is to courage what the winch is to the lever, a perpetual renewal of the point of support. Let the goal be on earth or in heaven, to reach the goal is everything; in the first case one is Columbus, in the second case, Jesus. Never to disobey the dictates of your conscience, never to allow your will to be disarmed, results in suffering, but in triumph as well. The propensity of mortals to fall does not preclude the possibility of soaring. From the fall comes the ascension. Weak souls are disconcerted by specious obstacles; strong souls, never. Perish they possibly may; conquer, they certainly will.

The decline of physical strength does not necessarily impair the will. Faith is only a secondary power;

the will is the first. The mountains, which faith is proverbially said to move are nothing in comparison with what the will can accomplish."

*160. Weigh well the thought of this; burn it into your brain cells; saturate your sinews with its strength; gain vitality and valor from its victorious message.

*161. The Conquering Chief MUST have huge endowment of Perseverance, unwavering decision, daring, and the fearless holding to the pathway of his goal—unswayed by the cheers or jeers of the mediocre multitude.

"Turn about. Take courage. Nature has a place for you if you are made of the right stuff. The masses that come and go, are melted over in the great melting-pot of nature; but those who rise up in their might with hearts of steel and souls of iron are never lost."

*162. If you will try to combine all that I have thus far said into an energetic, aggressive, intrepid plan of Action, you will experience the thrill of Power as you read the following classic from the great Victor Hugo (which you may interpret VICTOR, YOU GO).

"Human thought attains in certain men its maximum intensity.

The human mind has a summit.

This summit is the ideal.

"In each age three or four men of genius undertake the ascent. From below the world follows them with their eyes. These men go up the mountain, enter the clouds, disappear, reappear. People watch them, mark them. They walk by the side of precipices. A false step does not displease certain of the lookers-on. They daringly pursue their road. See them aloft, see them in the distance; they are but black specks. "How small they are," says the crowd. They are giants. On they go. The road is uneven, its difficulties constant. At each step a wall, at each step a trap. As they rise the cold increases. They must make their ladder, cut the ice and walk on it, hewing the steps in haste. Every storm is raging. Nevertheless they go forward in their madness. The air becomes difficult to breathe. The abyss increases around them. Some fall. Others stop and retrace their steps; there is a sad weariness.

"The bold ones continue; those predestined persist. The dreadful declivity sinks beneath and tries to draw them in; glory is treacherous. They are eyed by the eagles; the lightning plays about them; the hurricane is furious. No matter, they persevere."

They reach the pinnacle.
They are Super-men.
They are Conquering Chiefs.
Go you and profit by their example.